EXPLORING SCIENCE

MANIPULATING LIGHT

REFLECTION, REFRACTION, AND ABSORPTION

BY DARLENE R. STILLE

Content Adviser: Paul Ohmann, Ph.D., Assistant Professor of Physics,
University of St. Thomas, St. Paul, Minnesota

Science Adviser: Terrence E. Young Jr., M.Ed., M.L.S.,
Jefferson Parish (Louisiana) Public School System

Reading Adviser: Susan Kesselring, M.A., Literacy Educator,
Rosemount-Apple Valley-Eagan (Minnesota) School District

COMPASS POINT BOOKS • MINNEAPOLIS, MINNESOTA

Compass Point Books • 3109 West 50th Street, #115 • Minneapolis, MN 55410

Visit Compass Point Books on the Internet at *www.compasspointbooks.com*
or e-mail your request to *custserv@compasspointbooks.com*

Photographs ©: Tom Bean/Corbis, cover; Patrick Frischknecht/Peter Arndold, Inc., 4; Roger Ress-meyer/Corbis, 5, 26; Reuters/Corbis, 6; Martha McBride/Unicorn Stock Photos, 7; Steve Chenn/Corbis, 8; Eric Schaal/Time Life Pictures/Getty Images, 10; Bill & Sally Fletcher/ Tom Stack & Associates, Inc., 11; J. Lotter/Tom Stack & Associates, Inc., 14–15; Owen Franken/Corbis, 17; OneBlueShoe, 18, 27, 41; Judith Aronson/Peter Arnold, Inc., 19; Morton Beebe/Corbis, 20; Charles Krebs/Botanica/Getty Images, 23; Hulton Archive/Getty Images, 25; Craig Tuttle/Corbis, 28; Astrofoto/Peter Arnold, Inc., 29; Bo Zaunders/Corbis, 30; Thomas Kitchin/Tom Stack & Associates, Inc., 31; Richard Cummins/Corbis, 33; Tom Stewart/Corbis, 34; Philip Gould/Corbis, 36; Ron Watts/Corbis, 37; Troy Wayrynen/Columbian/NewSport/Corbis, 40; Stone/David Sutherland/Getty Images, 42; Taxi/Franz Camenzind/Getty Images, 43; William A. Bake/Corbis, 44; NASA/Roger Ress-meyer/Corbis, 46.

Editor: Nadia Higgins
Designer/Page Production: The Design Lab
Lead Designer: Jaime Martens
Photo Researcher: Marcie C. Spence
Illustrator: Farhana Hossain
Educational Consultant: Diane Smolinski

Managing Editor: Catherine Neitge
Creative Director: Keith Griffin
Editorial Director: Carol Jones

Library of Congress Cataloging-in-Publication Data
Stille, Darlene R.
    Manipulating light : reflection, refraction, and absorption / by Darlene R. Stille.
       p. cm. — (Exploring science)
    Includes bibliographical references and index.
    ISBN 0-7565-1258-1 (hardcover)
    1. Light—Juvenile literature. 2. Reflection (Optics)—Juvenile literature. 3. Refraction—Juvenile literature. 4. Light absorption—Juvenile literature. I. Title. II. Series:
Exploring science (Minneapolis, Minn.)
    QC360.S79 2006
    535—dc22   2005003903

About the Author

Darlene R. Stille is a science writer and author of more than 70 books for young people. When she was in high school, she fell in love with science. While attending the University of Illinois, she discovered that she also loved writing. She was fortunate enough to find a career as an editor and writer that allowed her to combine both of her interests. Darlene Stille now lives and writes in Michigan.

TABLE OF CONTENTS

CHAPTER ONE

How Light Behaves

A DANCER LOOKS at her image in a mirror while she practices a routine. A camper sees the beauty of stars twinkling in the nighttime sky. An artist examines the colors in a painting. A mirror image, twinkling stars, and colors are all possible because light behaves as waves. The way light waves bounce and bend shows details of objects around us.

HOW WAVES BOUNCE: REFLECTION

Bouncing waves are called reflections. When a ball hits a wall and bounces back, we could say that the ball is *reflected* back to us.

Waves of energy that hit objects are also reflected back. The waves might be light waves, sound waves, radio waves, or any other kind of wave.

Reflected light waves are some of the most important reflections. Reflected light comes from a source, such as the sun, a lamp, or a candle. The light from the source bounces off an object and into our eyes. We would not be able to see anything at all—trees, grass, desks, other people, and everything else in the world—without reflected light.

Sunlight bounces off a stand of rocks and hits the smooth surface of the water below. The light rays then bounce again, off the water and into our eyes, allowing us to see the spectacular reflection of rocks on water.

Sunlight Reflections

On a clear night, the moon shines brightly. Houses, trees, and cars faintly glow. They cast long, inky shadows on the nighttime landscape. And yet, the moon is not a source of light itself. What we see as moonlight is really sunlight reflected off the moon.

Planets, asteroids, and comets, like the moon, do not give off much light of their own. We see them because they reflect light from the sun. The sun, like other stars, glows because nuclear (atomic) reactions inside it make it hot enough to shine.

Halley's comet is a ball made mostly of ice, dust, and rock that orbits the sun. Like all comets, Halley's comet is visible because of reflected sunlight. Last seen in 1986, the comet appears in the sky about every 76 years.

The moon and planets are opaque objects, which means they block out light. Light is reflected off only one side of these objects, the side facing the sun. As a result, the moon and planets cast shadows. These shadows can create beautiful effects in the sky called lunar and solar eclipses.

When the moon passes through Earth's shadow, part or all of the moon's surface grows darker. This event is called a lunar eclipse. The sun, moon, and Earth must be perfectly lined up in order for a lunar eclipse to occur. Earth must be between the sun and the moon in order to block the sun's rays.

During a lunar eclipse, the moon does not look totally dark. Some of the sun's rays bend around Earth and give the moon a reddish color.

An eclipse of the sun occurs when the moon is between the sun and Earth. The moon's shadow passes across Earth, totally or partially blocking out the sun.

Every year, at least two solar eclipses are visible from various places on Earth. The type of solar eclipse shown here is an annular eclipse. The moon darkens the middle of the sun, leaving a bright ring around the edges.

HOW WAVES BEND: REFRACTION

Bending waves are called refractions. Like reflection, refraction can occur with any kind of wave. *Refracted* waves do not bounce back. Instead, they continue going forward, but in a new direction. As with reflected light waves, refracted light waves help us see things.

Refraction in our eyes focuses light waves so that our eyes see objects clearly. In eyeglass lenses, refraction helps correct vision problems. In a camera lens, it focuses an image to make a photograph. Refraction even causes the rainbow that arches across the sky at the end of a thunderstorm.

DID YOU KNOW?

MOON HALOS

A fuzzy-looking ring of light, called a halo, sometimes appears around the moon, especially on a cold winter night. The moon does not actually have a ring around it. Light rays reflected off the moon and refracted by ice crystals in the atmosphere create the illusion of a halo.

SOAKING LIGHT IN: ABSORPTION

Not all waves bend or bounce when they hit a surface. These waves get taken up, or absorbed, by the object. Special tiles or heavy drapes can absorb sound waves, muffling sound. Opaque materials that you cannot see through, such as wood or wool, can absorb light waves.

Reflection, refraction, and absorption are the main ways in which light waves behave. These behaviors of light allow us to see the objects in the world—and even in outer space.

As a skateboarder flies in front of a green brick wall, his body absorbs light rays coming toward him. Like all opaque objects, his body blocks out light, casting a shadow behind it.

CHAPTER TWO

The Law of Reflection

REFLECTED LIGHT WAVES do not bounce back from a surface in any old way. They follow a strict pattern called the law of reflection.

HOW LIGHT TRAVELS

We can think of light as being made of billions of tiny rays. All these rays travel in a straight line, and they all travel parallel to each other. The leading edge of these billions of rays is called a wave front.

Light rays travel in a straight line from a source, such as the sun, until they strike an object. What happens next depends on what the object is made of. The rays behave one way if they strike a smooth mirror and another way if they strike a rough concrete sidewalk. The way light rays bounce off an object allows us to see that objects are made of different materials with different textures.

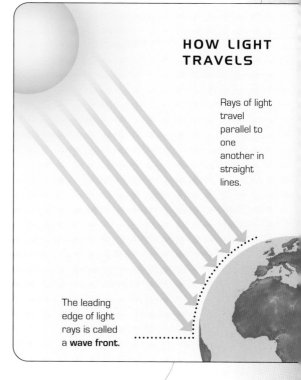

HOW LIGHT TRAVELS

Rays of light travel parallel to one another in straight lines.

The leading edge of light rays is called a **wave front.**

How Light Rays Travel Through Space

Waves are energy that travels through a medium. The medium is the material the waves travel *through*. Sound waves travel through air. Water waves travel through water. What does starlight travel through?

For centuries, this question puzzled scientists. There is almost no matter in outer space. Scientists think of space as being a vacuum. So how does light from distant stars and galaxies reach our

eyes on Earth?

In 1905, German-born American physicist Albert Einstein came up with an answer: Light isn't necessarily a wave. It can behave like a particle as well as like a wave. This particle of light is called a photon.

In Einstein's view, a photon is actually a tiny bundle of energy. All photons travel in straight lines, and the straight paths taken by photons form rays of light. Photons travel great distances over space to reach Earth.

Astronomers measure distances in space in terms of light-

In 1921, Albert Einstein (1879–1955) earned the most prestigious award in physics—the Nobel Prize—for his ideas about light.

years, or how far a photon travels in the vacuum of space in one year. Photons are the fastest things in the entire universe. In a vacuum, they travel about 12 million times faster than a car on the highway. One light-year is so long, it is practically unimaginable. One light-year is 5.88 trillion miles (9.46 trillion kilometers).

The closest star to Earth is about four light-years away. It would take a spacecraft traveling at the speed of light four years to reach this star. Because light must travel vast distances over the universe, we are seeing stars as they were when the light left them. If a star or other object is 10 billion light-years away, we are seeing that object as it was 10 billion years ago. That is how long it took the photons of light to reach Earth. So, the farther out our telescopes can look in space, the farther back they look in time.

The nearest galaxy, Andromeda, is about 2 million light-years away. That means it would take a spacecraft moving at the speed of light 2 million years to reach this neighboring galaxy.

THE ANGLES OF RAYS

Understanding how reflected light behaves is a matter of "knowing the angles." To understand the angles, we need to imagine a single light ray striking a surface. This is the incidence ray. The light ray bouncing off the surface is the reflected ray.

ANGLES OF LIGHT RAYS

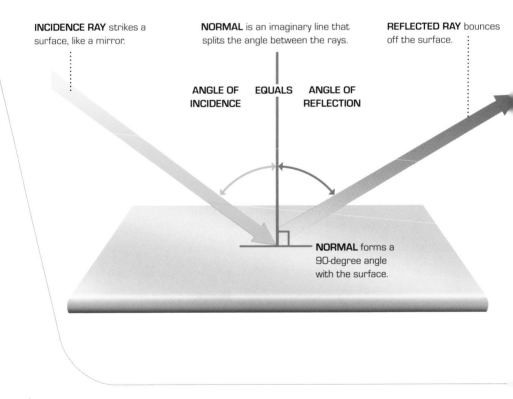

INCIDENCE RAY strikes a surface, like a mirror.

NORMAL is an imaginary line that splits the angle between the rays.

REFLECTED RAY bounces off the surface.

ANGLE OF   EQUALS   ANGLE OF
INCIDENCE   REFLECTION

NORMAL forms a 90-degree angle with the surface.

Now we need to imagine another line going straight toward a surface. The surface can be anything—a flower petal, a tree, a mirror, or someone's nose. This imaginary line is perpendicular to the surface at the point where the incidence ray strikes the surface. At this point, it makes a 90-degree angle with the surface. Scientists call this imaginary line the "normal line" or "the normal."

The normal is right between the incidence ray and the reflected ray. It splits the angle between the two, creating the angle of incidence and the angle of reflection. According to the law of reflection, the angle of reflection will always be equal to the angle of incidence.

SMOOTH AND ROUGH SURFACES

Why is the law of reflection important? Because it explains why smooth and rough surfaces look different. We know that the angle of incidence is always equal to the angle of reflection. Therefore, reflected light rays travel in different paths depending on the texture of the surface they strike.

Why can we see our reflection in a smooth, shiny surface, such as a bathroom mirror or a polished piece of metal? When rays from a light source strike a smooth, shiny surface, all the rays reflect off in the same direction, allowing us to see a mirror image.

Light reflects off smooth surfaces, such as still water, in the same direction, allowing us to see reflections. Light reflects off rough surfaces, such as trees and mountains, in many directions.

Why can't we see our reflection in a rough surface, such as a concrete sidewalk or a piece of wood? What about a smooth, dull surface, such as a piece of writing paper? Because the surfaces of all these objects are uneven—including the sheet of paper. Although the paper looks and feels smooth, under a microscope, it appears rough and bumpy. In contrast, a mirror or piece of polished metal looks smooth even under a microscope.

The angle of reflection must equal the angle of incidence, so the light rays striking

When rays
of light strike
a smooth
surface, like
a mirror . . .

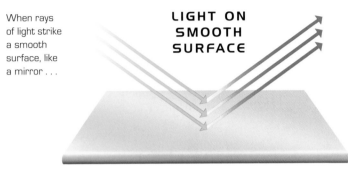

**LIGHT ON
SMOOTH
SURFACE**

. . . all the
rays reflect
off in the
same
direction.

When rays
of light strike
a rough
surface, like
a concrete
sidewalk . . .

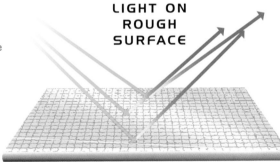

**LIGHT ON
ROUGH
SURFACE**

. . . the rays
reflect off in
different
directions.

an uneven surface reflect off in different directions. For example, the bumps in a concrete sidewalk have surfaces that slant in different ways. Because the surfaces slant, the angles of incidence vary as light strikes them. That means the angles of reflection must vary as well. Because of the differing angles at which the light is reflected to our eyes, we see a sidewalk as being rough.

CHAPTER THREE

Mirrors: Reflected Light Rays

MIRRORS CAN BE MADE of highly polished metal or other smooth material. Most manufactured mirrors are made by putting a thin coating of silver or aluminum on the back of a sheet of glass.

The smoother the surface, the sharper and clearer the reflected image. There are three basic kinds of mirrors—plane, convex, and concave. Each type creates a different kind of image.

PLANE MIRRORS

We are most familiar with the plane, or flat, mirrors in bathrooms and dressing rooms. The image in a plane mirror is the same size as the reflected body, face, or other object. It is right-side up. Left and right, however, are reversed in a plane-mirror image. That's why words on a T-shirt read backward in a reflection.

When you look at yourself in a mirror, your image seems to be standing behind the mirror. That's because of the way the light rays reflect. The light rays appear to focus, or meet, at a point behind the mirror surface.

An image is reversed in a plane mirror. Here, the baby touches the mirror with his right hand. In the image, the left hand is reaching out.

CONVEX MIRRORS

A convex mirror is curved slightly outward like the underside of a spoon or shallow bowl. As in a plane mirror, the image is upright and seems to be on the other side of the mirror, or behind the mirror surface. But there are two main differences between the images in plane and convex mirrors.

First, the image in a convex mirror is not the same size as the reflected object. The image in a convex mirror is smaller than the reflected object. Second, the view in a convex mirror is wider than the view in a plane mirror. We can see a lot more of an area because of the way that light is reflected in a convex mirror.

Convex mirrors can be very useful in everyday life. Most cars have side-view mirrors on the passenger side that are convex mirrors. Drivers can see more of the road behind them and cars approaching on the right-hand side.

Convex mirrors on cars carry a warning: "Objects in mirror are closer than they appear."

FUN HOUSE MIRRORS

Fun house mirrors reflect images that are distorted. The mirror surfaces are curved in such ways that the reflected light rays make images of people appear to be much shorter and fatter or taller and thinner than the people really are.

CONCAVE MIRRORS

Hold the inside of a spoon up to your face, and look at your reflection. You are upside-down.

A concave mirror curves inward like a spoon. Reflected rays from the inward curves of a concave mirror can produce a variety of effects, depending on how far the reflected object is from the mirror surface. The light rays might focus so that an image appears to be behind the mirror or in front of the mirror. The image might be right-side up or upside-down. The image might be smaller than the reflected object, or bigger.

Light rays reflected from an object close to a concave mirror can magnify the object. Common cosmetic magnifying mirrors are concave mirrors. They make your face look bigger than it really is.

Concave mirrors can concentrate light rays from objects that are far away. For example, the sun is very far away. The focused rays of sunlight reflected from a small concave mirror can produce enough heat to set a piece of paper or a stick of wood on fire. Concave mirrors are used to concentrate energy from the sun in a solar furnace. A solar furnace directs the focused beams to heat a container of fluid, such as water or oil.

Solar energy panels on a solar furnace form a giant concave mirror. Notice that the reflected image of sky and grass is upside-down. The blue sky is at the bottom of the image, and the green grass is at the top.

THREE TYPES OF MIRRORS

Different kinds of mirrors form images differently.

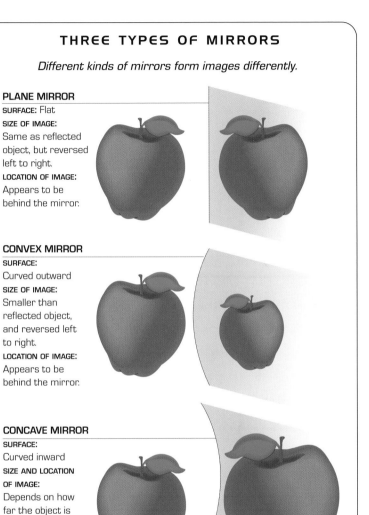

PLANE MIRROR
SURFACE: Flat
SIZE OF IMAGE:
Same as reflected object, but reversed left to right.
LOCATION OF IMAGE:
Appears to be behind the mirror.

CONVEX MIRROR
SURFACE:
Curved outward
SIZE OF IMAGE:
Smaller than reflected object, and reversed left to right.
LOCATION OF IMAGE:
Appears to be behind the mirror.

CONCAVE MIRROR
SURFACE:
Curved inward
SIZE AND LOCATION OF IMAGE:
Depends on how far the object is from the mirror. Image can be reversed left to right or top to bottom.

Kaleidoscope: Beauty in Reflections

It can be a toy or a work of art. Either way, kaleidoscopes are objects that some people collect as a hobby. The word *kaleidoscope* comes from Greek words meaning "beautiful form to see."

The basic kaleidoscope is a tube containing at least two mirrors set at angles to one another. The tube is closed at both ends. The mirrors can be made of glass, Plexiglas (a kind of see-through plastic), or polished metal.

Inside the tube are bits of colored glass, colored oil, dried flowers, or just about anything that will make an interesting image in the mirrors. At one end is an eyepiece to look through. The contents of the tube reflect from one mirror to another, making beautiful, symmetrical patterns. The patterns can look like multicolored stars with many points or like stained glass windows. When the tube is turned, the contents become mixed, creating a different set of reflected patterns.

The kaleidoscope was invented in 1816 by a Scottish genius named Sir David Brewster. He studied the science of light and invented many scientific instruments, but he is best remembered for the kaleidoscope. The kaleidoscope quickly became all the rage. Manufacturers made hundreds of thousands of the reflecting tubes. Sir David Brewster patented the kaleidoscope in 1817, but he never made any money from his wonderful invention.

Simple green leaves in a kaleidoscope formed this beautiful pattern.

REFLECTION AND REFRACTION IN TELESCOPES

Telescopes help astronomers see distant stars and galaxies by making these objects seem closer than they are. Telescopes that reflect or refract visible light waves are called optical telescopes. Most optical telescopes today are reflecting telescopes, but the first telescopes were refractors.

Italian scientist Galileo Galilei did not invent the optical telescope, but he was the first to make important discoveries using telescopes. In the early 1600s, Galileo built and used refracting telescopes. They were long, narrow tubes with curved lenses inside that bent and focused light from planets and stars. He found mountains and craters on the moon and discovered four moons around Jupiter.

English physicist Sir Isaac Newton in 1668 invented the reflecting telescope. His telescope used a plane mirror and a concave mirror in a tube to collect and focus light from stars and planets.

As time went on, astronomers needed better and better telescopes to magnify distant objects and show them in finer detail. The level of detail of an image is called its resolution. The larger the mirror and the longer the tube, the better the resolution these early telescopes had. British astronomer Sir William Herschel in the 1700s used a reflecting telescope with a mirror 4 feet (1.2 meters) in diameter in a 40-foot-long

(12-m) tube. He discovered the planet Uranus in 1781 and also found galaxies beyond our Milky Way galaxy.

The Hubble Space Telescope is a modern reflecting telescope in orbit around Earth. Since it is in space, it avoids the

Italian scientist Galileo Galilei (1564–1642) built larger and more powerful telescopes than those that had been in use before.

blurring caused by Earth's atmosphere refracting light from the stars. The main mirror of the Hubble is 94 inches (2.4 m) in diameter.

The world's largest optical telescopes are two identical reflecting telescopes at the Keck Observatory on the island of Hawaii. Each telescope has 36 mirrors that work together as one huge mirror, with a total diameter of 33 feet (10 m).

The Keck I telescope collects light waves from outer space. Notice the silhouettes of two people underneath the telescope on the right. This gives a sense of the telescope's enormous size.

CHAPTER FOUR

Refraction

STANDING IN A POOL on a hot, summer day, you look down. Your legs look different—shorter than you know they are. This illusion is created by refraction, or bending light. What causes light to bend? It has to do with how light changes as it passes through one material into another.

CHANGING SPEEDS OF LIGHT

Light rays can travel through water and other see-through, or transparent, material. However, light travels through different materials at different speeds. It travels fastest through a vacuum, an area that is a completely empty space. There is no matter—not even air—inside a vacuum.

At the boundary between air and water, light rays change speed and bend. Here, refracted rays make the straw look as though it is broken.

The more matter there is in a material, the slower light will travel through it. How much matter is packed into a material is called its density. A gas, such as air, is not as dense as a liquid, such as water. And water is less dense than most solids, such as a piece of glass. So light rays travel through air almost as fast as through a vacuum. They travel faster through air than through water, and faster through water than through glass.

Look closely to see the upside-down image of a red barn refracted in tiny dew drops.

WHY STARS TWINKLE

Earth's atmosphere is made up of layers and pockets of hotter and colder air. Hotter air is less dense than colder air. These pockets and layers constantly move around. The movement of these air pockets and layers is called atmospheric turbulence. As light from a distant star passes through the atmosphere, the changes in the density of the air pockets and layers refract the rays. The turbulence causes starlight passing through the atmosphere to bend in one direction and then another. Our eyes see the bending as a twinkling of the light.

When a light ray goes from air through the surface of a more dense material, such as glass or water, it slows down. Any change in speed, either speeding up or slowing down, is what causes the light rays to refract. The greater the change in speed, the more the rays will bend.

Bending light rays in a glass create varying images of this man's face.

Mirages: Illusions from Refraction

The driver of a car going down a highway on a hot summer day sees a pool of water on the pavement in the distance. The passengers in the car see it, too. As the car gets closer to the pool, the water disappears or moves to a place farther ahead on the road. There really was no pool of water. What the people in the car saw was an optical illusion called a mirage.

Mirages are caused by the refraction, or bending, of light rays. Light rays travel at different speeds through different materials. Temperature changes in a material, such as air, can cause changes in the density of the material. Changes in density can slow down or speed up a ray of light. This is what causes a mirage.

Heat from the sun makes the air near the ground warmer and therefore less dense than the air above it. As light rays pass from cool air above to warmer air below, they speed up. This change in speed causes the rays to refract, or bend. In addition, the warmer and cooler layers of air are mixing together. As the light rays pass through this churning air, the rays appear to wiggle. The wiggling creates the optical illusion of waves on water.

In a sense, mirages are real because light rays are real. A camera can take an image of a mirage, such as this one of water in the distance.

HOW MIRAGES ARE FORMED

*A mirage is the deceptive appearance of a
distant object caused by refraction of light.*

1 Heat from
the sun makes
the air near the
ground warmer
than the air above it.

2 Light rays—passing from cooler to
warmer air—speed up and appear to
wiggle. They refract, or bend
upward, before reaching
the ground.

3 The
refracted
rays create an
image of the sky
on the ground. The
wiggling creates the
illusion of waves on water.

Mirages of water appear above desert sands. They can also
appear over big lakes and oceans and over fields of snow or ice.
Layers of warm and cool air high in the atmosphere can cause
spectacular mirages. Lights rays reflected from distant objects
such as ships or rocks can refract at the boundary between
dense, cool air and less dense, warm air. The refracted rays can
cause mirages that look like ships, rocks, or buildings floating in
the sky.

REFRACTION IN THE EYE

Refraction is crucial to vision. Light rays reflect off objects and travel to the eye in straight lines. However, these light rays cannot come together to form images on their own. Our eyes have clear lenses that refract light. Each lens bends light rays so that they focus on the retina at the back of the eye, creating clear images of the objects.

Vision problems occur when the natural lens does not focus the rays properly. When the rays focus in front of the retina, this causes nearsightedness—near objects look clear, but distant objects look blurry. When the rays hit the retina before they are in focus, this causes farsightedness—distant objects look clear, but near objects look blurry.

A camera lens refracts colorful lights from a Ferris wheel. The lens works much the same way as the lens of the eye. The camera lens focuses light rays to make an image on film or a digital image on a memory card.

Eyeglass lenses and contact lenses correct vision problems by refracting light rays so that they focus properly on the retina. Lenses that are thicker at the edges and thinner in the center correct nearsightedness. These lenses are called negative lenses. Lenses that are thicker at the center than at the edges correct farsightedness. These lenses are called positive lenses.

Both positive and negative lenses bend light because of the difference in thickness. The speed of the light changes inside the lens. Rays going through the thicker parts of the lens must travel farther through this dense material than rays going through the thinner parts. This has the effect of slowing the speed of the rays going through the thicker parts. The change in speed refracts the rays, and the bending causes the rays to focus.

During an eye exam, a woman looks through a series of different lenses, hoping to find the one that best corrects her vision.

HOW WE SEE USING REFRACTION

Our eyes focus light reflected by objects to form images.

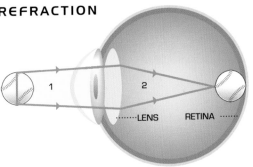

NORMAL VISION

1 Light reflected from an object enters the eye in straight lines.
2 The lens bends the light rays and focuses them on the retina to form images.

For many people with nearsightedness and farsightedness, the natural lens does not focus light rays properly, and the images appear blurry.

NEARSIGHTED VISION

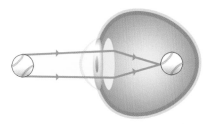

Light rays focus in front of the retina. Near objects look clear, but distant objects look blurry. This can be caused by an eyeball that is too long or a lens that focuses light too much.

CORRECTING NEARSIGHTEDNESS

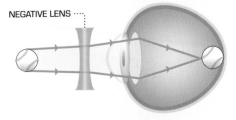

Negative lenses can correct nearsightednness by spreading out light rays before they hit the eye lens. The lens can focus the image farther out, placing it correctly on the retina.

FARSIGHTED VISION

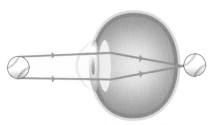

Light rays focus behind the retina. Distant objects look clear, but near objects look blurry. This can be caused by an eyeball that is too short or a lens that cannot focus light enough.

CORRECTING FARSIGHTEDNESS

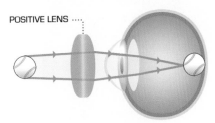

Positive lenses can correct farsightednness by slightly bringing together light rays before they hit the eye lens. The lens can focus the image closer in, placing it correctly on the retina.

CHAPTER FIVE

Absorption

WE KNOW THAT light can bend and bounce when it strikes a surface. Often, however, some or most of the rays striking a surface are absorbed by the material. The material sucks up light the way a paper towel sucks up water. The absorption of light is very important to how we see things.

TRANSPARENT, OPAQUE, TRANSLUCENT

Absorption explains why some materials are see-through and others aren't. Imagine shining a flashlight at a piece of glass, a thick blanket, and a sheet of waxed paper. Light rays can go right through transparent materials, such as glass. They can be absorbed by opaque materials, such as a blanket. There are even some translucent materials, like waxed paper, that absorb some light rays and let others pass through. We can see fuzzy images, but no details, through waxed paper and other translucent materials such as frosted glass or plastic.

Sunlight is absorbed by the opaque window frame but passes through the transparent glass, creating a pattern of shadow and light behind it.

Tinted glass or plastic are translucent materials used to make lenses for sunglasses. The lenses are covered by special colored coatings. The common colors for tinted glass are gray, brown, and green. The coating does not blur images, but acts like a filter to absorb, or block out, some light rays from the sun. The tint reduces glare (the amount of light reaching your eyes). The darker the color, the more rays it blocks out.

Some coatings also block out the sun's ultraviolet rays. You cannot see these powerful rays, but they can damage your eyes.

SEEING COLORS

The grass is green, a shirt is red, and jeans are blue. Why do we perceive the world as being made of many colors? The answer has to do with both absorption and reflection—and the properties of light itself.

Translucent materials don't have to be man-made. Delicate maple leaves absorb some light and let some pass through.

Sunlight streams through a window, making a bright, warm square on the floor. The light looks white. White sunlight, however, is made up of many different colors of light. The colors—red, orange, yellow, green, blue, and violet—combine to form sunlight.

What makes red light red and violet light violet? The answer is wave frequency.

We can think of light rays as a series of up-and-down waves like the ones pictured in the diagram below. Imagine that you could stand in one spot and watch the waves traveling past you. You could see how often, or frequently, the waves go by, counting how many complete waves pass in a certain amount of time. This measurement would be the light's frequency.

WAVES

Each color in white light has its own frequency. Red has the lowest frequency; violet has the highest. The others are in between. All the waves together are called the color spectrum, or the visible spectrum.

So what is happening when we look at colored materials around us? We do not actually see colors in the materials themselves. Depending on the chemicals inside them, materials absorb some colors of light and reflect others. What we see is certain colors of light waves reflected from these materials.

A shirt appears red, for example, because chemicals in the cloth absorb all the waves of light except red. Red gets reflected. When the reflected red light reaches our eyes, impulses go to our brain, which tells us that we are seeing red.

VISIBLE SPECTRUM

Visible light is made up of different colors, each with a different frequency.

| COLOR ▶ Violet | Blue | | Green | Yellow | Orange | Red |

FREQUENCY ▶

Highest ·· Lowest

White shirts, white sheets, or white tablecloths are objects that reflect almost all the waves of the light that strikes them. We see all the reflected waves of light together as white. When something looks black, it is absorbing almost all the waves that strike it.

Light is what lets us tell the difference between colors in team uniforms. The colors we see are created by certain wavelengths of light reflecting off the fabric.

What about colors such as pink, turquoise, or brown? These colors are not in the visible spectrum. They occur when colors mix. A flamingo looks pink, for example, because its feathers reflect all the colors in the spectrum (white) with a little more red.

DID YOU KNOW?

BLUE SKIES

When light rays strike tiny particles such as molecules, the rays bounce off in different directions. This bouncing effect is called scattering. On a clear day, the sky looks blue because molecules in the air scatter more blue rays than other colors toward our eyes.

Prisms and Rainbows

A diamond ring flashes in a jewelry store showcase. The crystal pendants on a chandelier sparkle when the chandelier lights are turned on. A rainbow arches across the sky as the sun peeks out from behind storm clouds. Diamonds, crystal pendants, and rainbows all can show us the colors that make up white light.

English physicist Sir Isaac Newton discovered that white

light is made up of many colors. He used specially shaped pieces of glass called prisms to study light and color in the late 1600s and early 1700s. A prism has three or more flat sides. Diamonds for jewelry and glass for chandeliers are cut into shapes that form prisms. Newton watched as light passing through a prism broke up into many colors.

A prism works by refracting light waves passing through it. Each color bends at its own angle. Red waves bend the least, and violet waves bend the

As pure white light passes through a prism, it is split apart, revealing the rainbow colors of the visible spectrum. Not all light is made up of these same colors, however. Prisms are useful parts of instruments that measure the composition of various kinds of light.

most. Newton's studies with prisms led him to conclude that what we perceive as color in objects is different colors of light reaching our eyes.

All the colors of the rainbow come from refracted light. In rainbows, it is raindrops that do the refracting. The raindrops act as tiny prisms. The outer edge of a rainbow is red, and the inner edge is violet. Orange, yellow, green, and other colors blend into one another in between.

Sometimes two rainbows form together. The secondary rainbow (left) forms when light waves bend twice inside the raindrops. The order of the colors in a secondary rainbow is the reverse of the primary rainbow.

It's easy to understand how light lets us see. Turn off a light, and everything goes black. Turn it back on, and the room appears again. But light's story is much more complex than that. As light bends, bounces, and is absorbed, it shows the details of the objects around us. As it reflects, light shows the textures of water, wood, gold, wool, and everything else. As it refracts inside our eyes, light forms images our brains can understand. As it is absorbed, light creates shadows and lets us see colors. All around us, light reveals the richness and variety of our world.

Sunlight passes through a dome with stained glass windows, creating a rich visual display.

angle—geometric space, measured in degrees, between two lines that meet at one point

concave mirror—a mirror that curves inward, like the inside of a bowl

convex mirror—a mirror that curves outward, like the outside of a bowl

density—how tightly packed matter is inside an object; feathers have low density, while lead has high density

focus—to bring light waves together so they meet at a single point, producing clear images

frequency—the number of complete waves going past a point in a certain amount of time

incidence ray—ray or beam of light coming from a source toward a surface

lens—a piece of curved glass or plastic in eyeglasses, a camera, or a telescope that refracts light to focus or magnify images; also the clear part of the eye that focuses light

molecules—tiny units of matter made up of two or more atoms

opaque—not see-through; blocking all rays of light

perpendicular—straight up and down relative to another surface; the two lines that form the letter T are perpendicular to each other

photon—particle of light

reflected ray—ray of light bouncing off a surface, such as a mirror

refracted ray—ray of light bending as it goes from one material into another

translucent—partially see-through; allowing some rays of light to pass through

transparent—see-through; allowing all rays of light to pass through

vacuum—a space that is completely empty of all matter, including air and other gases

visible spectrum—light rays that can be seen, ranging in color from red to violet

waves—energy moving through a medium, such as water or air

▶ There are some frequencies of light that our eyes cannot see. Infrared light has a frequency just lower than that of red light, and ultraviolet light's frequency is just higher than that of violet light. We can feel infrared rays as heat. We need to protect ourselves from ultraviolet rays, which can cause sunburn and maybe even skin cancer.

▶ Other kinds of waves can also be refracted. Refracted sound waves allow sound to travel farther at night than during the day. Cool air near the ground at nighttime is denser than warmer air higher up. At the surface between the warmer and cooler air, the sound waves are refracted. The refraction sends the sound waves at an angle that allows them to be heard farther away.

▶ All substances give off light if they become hot enough. Every substance gives off its own unique pattern of light. Scientists use instruments called spectrometers to analyze this light. The spectrometer spreads out the light from the object into a spectrum, or band of colors. By studying light from distant stars, astronomers can tell what substances are in the stars.

▶ Reflected light waves influence what colors we see, but the way our eyes and brains interpret light have a lot to do with what we see as well. Sometimes our eyes can fool us. Stare at a red apple for 30 seconds. Then immediately look at a white sheet of paper. You will continue to see the shape of the apple, but the apple will be green. Look at a red apple against a black background. Then look at it against a white background. The apple seems lighter in front of the black background and darker against a white background.

The Hubble Space Telescope was launched into orbit around Earth in 1990. Soon after, scientists discovered that its mirror had a problem. The light it reflected produced images that were slightly blurred. Engineers designed—and space shuttle astronauts installed—a device that acted as "eyeglasses" for Hubble. The device refracted the reflected light so that it focused properly to produce clear images.

At the Library

Burton, Jane, and Kim Taylor. *The Nature and Science of Reflections*. Milwaukee, Wis.: Gareth Stevens, 2001.

Gardner, Robert. *Experiments with Light and Mirrors*. Springfield, N.J.: Enslow, 1995.

Orr, Tamra. *The Telescope*. New York: Franklin Watts, 2004.

Riley, Peter D. *Light and Color*. North Mankato, Minn.: Smart Apple Media, 2005.

On the Webd

For more information on light, use FactHound to track down Web sites related to this book.

1. Go to *www.facthound.com*
2. Type in a search word related to this book or this book ID: **0756512581**
3. Click on the *Fetch It* button.

FactHound will find the best Web sites for you.

On the Road

Mount Wilson Observatory
Mount Wilson, CA 91023
626/440-9016
www.mtwilson.edu
To visit one of the oldest and most prestigious astronomical observatories, which houses two giant reflecting telescopes

Museum of Science
Science Park
Boston, MA 02114
617/723-2500
www.mos.org
To explore interactive exhibits about color, mirrors, optical illusions, and other science topics

National Renewable Energy Laboratory (NREL)
1617 Cole Blvd.
Golden, CO 80401-3393
303/275-3000
www.nrel.gov
To learn about giant mirrors that collect and focus light rays from the sun

Explore all the books in this series

Chemical Change
From Fireworks to Rust

Erosion
How Land Forms, How It Changes

Manipulating Light
Reflection, Refraction, and Absorption

Minerals
From Apatite to Zinc

Natural Resources
Using and Protecting Earth's Supplies

Physical Change
Reshaping Matter

Soil
Digging Into Earth's Vital Resource

Waves
Energy on the Move